COLFAX

Dear Parent:
Your child's love of reading starts here!

Every child learns to read in a different way and at his or her own speed. Some go back and forth between reading levels and read favorite books again and again. Others read through each level in order. You can help your young reader improve and become more confident by encouraging his or her own interests and abilities. From books your child reads with you to the first books he or she reads alone, there are I Can Read Books for every stage of reading:

SHARED READING
Basic language, word repetition, and whimsical illustrations, ideal for sharing with your emergent reader

BEGINNING READING
Short sentences, familiar words, and simple concepts for children eager to read on their own

READING WITH HELP
Engaging stories, longer sentences, and language play for developing readers

READING ALONE
Complex plots, challenging vocabulary, and high-interest topics for the independent reader

ADVANCED READING
Short paragraphs, chapters, and exciting themes for the perfect bridge to chapter books

I Can Read Books have introduced children to the joy of reading since 1957. Featuring award-winning authors and illustrators and a fabulous cast of beloved characters, I Can Read Books set the standard for beginning readers.

A lifetime of discovery begins with the magical words "I Can Read!"

Visit www.icanread.com for information
on enriching your child's reading experience.

For the brand-newest
O'Connor
—J.O'C.

For Rick Whipple
—R.P.G.

I Can Read Book® is a trademark of HarperCollins Publishers.

JoJo and the Twins
Text copyright © 2018 by Jane O'Connor
Illustrations copyright © 2018 by Robin Preiss Glasser
All rights reserved. Manufactured in U.S.A.
No part of this book may be used or reproduced in any manner whatsoever without written permission except in the case
of brief quotations embodied in critical articles and reviews. For information address HarperCollins Children's Books,
a division of HarperCollins Publishers, 195 Broadway, New York, NY 10007.
www.icanread.com

Library of Congress Control Number: 2018934060
ISBN 978-0-06-237805-7 (trade bdg.) —ISBN 978-0-06-237804-0 (pbk.)
18 19 20 21 22 LSC 10 9 8 7 6 5 4 3 2 1 ❖ First Edition

I Can Read!™

JOJO
AND THE
TWINS

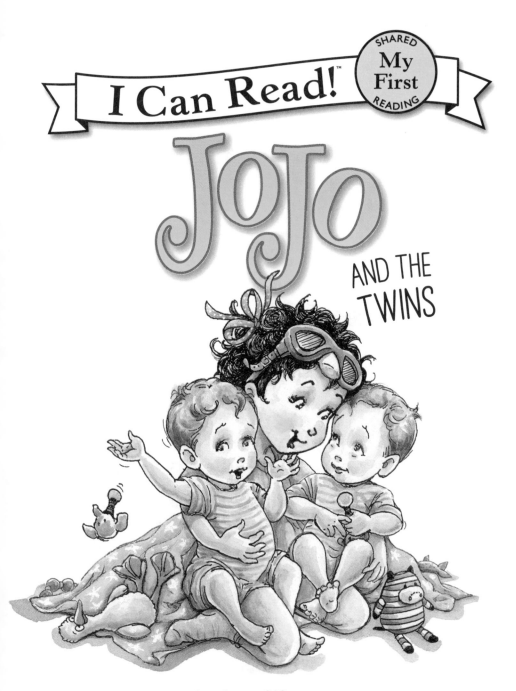

by Jane O'Connor
pictures by Robin Preiss Glasser

HARPER
An Imprint of HarperCollinsPublishers

Hi! I am JoJo.

I am Nancy's little sister.

6

But now I am a big sister too!
See how little my brothers are.

Robby and Teddy are twins.

My twins look just the same.

Robby and Teddy cry the same.

They burp the same.

They even sleep the same.

It's easy to mix them up.

12

"Is that Robby?" I ask.

"No, it's Teddy," Daddy says.

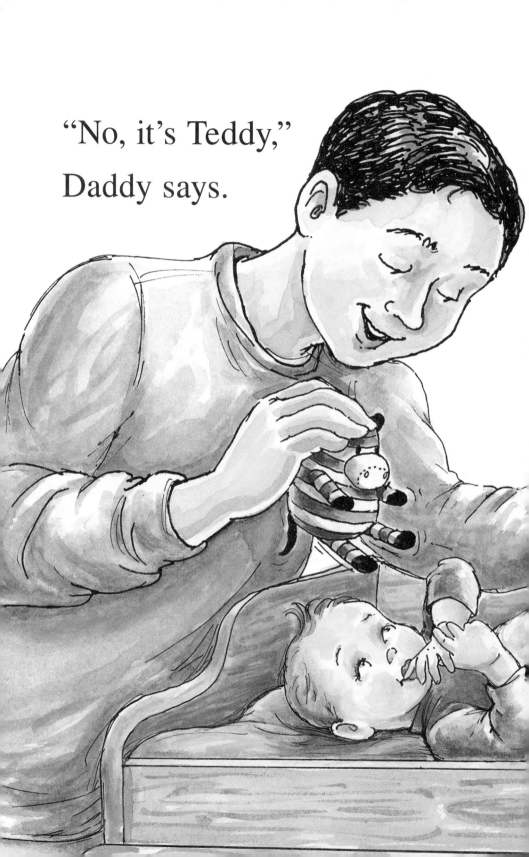

"Teddy has a pink dot
on his fanny.
Robby does not."

"We need a better way
to tell the twins apart,"
Mommy says.

So I think hard.

"I know!"

I run and get my markers.

The twins are asleep.
I climb on a chair
by the crib.

Mommy runs in.

"JoJo! What are you doing?"

"I will put an *R*
on Robby's head,
and a *T* on Teddy's head.
Then we won't mix them up!"

"No, JoJo,"
Mommy says.
"We need another way."

So I think harder.

Maybe stickers.

Maybe stamps.

Maybe headbands.

What do Mommy and Daddy say?

"No, no, and no!"

"But you are a good big sister.

You love the twins."

Yes! I am a good big sister.

I sing for the twins.

I dance for the twins.

I make funny faces for them.

But Robby and Teddy
just stare back at me.

Then one day
I make lots of silly noises
and the twins smile—
their first smiles ever!

"Look! Look!
I made the twins smile,"
I shout.

"Their smiles are not the same!
Now we can tell the twins apart."

It is simple.

Robby has a dimple.

Teddy does not.

I am a good big sister
and a smart one too!